HENRY SIMON

Mary and Leigh Block Gallery, Northwestern University
September 19—December 7, 1997

LIZ SEATON

1901-1995

Henry Simon: 1901-1995 is
published to accompany an
exhibition of the same title on
view at the Mary and Leigh
Block Gallery, Northwestern
University, September 19
through December 7, 1997.

Distributed by
Northwestern University Press.

Design by Diane Jaroch.

ISBN 0-941680-18-5

Cover image:
Detail from *Bishop McKendree
and His Escorts at Lebanon*
by Henry Simon, 1940, casein
on gesso with oil glazes (see
plate 5, page xiii).

Contents

Acknowledgments

David Mickenberg

Director,

Mary and Leigh Block Gallery

It is the nature of scholarship to bring the past to the present, to perpetuate a process of interpretation that provides an ever expanding understanding of the influences and circumstances that give rise to history. Within this process, the museum has the opportunity to restore to the historical discourse those artists marginalized by time, location and circumstance. Museums have been criticized for decontextualizing art. But their presentation and publication of the work of many of the artists born early in this century does just the opposite. Recognition and interpretation of the political, social and aesthetic ideas and characteristics of these artists has substantially aided our understanding of the complexity and diversity of the first half of this century.

It is therefore with great pride and excitement that we present this retrospective of the work of Henry Simon. From his youth until his death in 1995 Henry Simon reflected the varied American experience while speaking with a voice that was unique and special to the Midwest. As Liz Seaton's article clearly portrays, Simon's *oeuvre* can be seen as a reflection of the issues and ideas which concerned so many in a time of personal redefinition and vast societal change. That we are able to present his work spanning his entire adult life is a tribute to the support of family and friends and the wisdom of many who brought to our attention the importance of this artist.

Every exhibition is a collaborative effort in which the expertise and creativity of many is allowed to shine. The Block Gallery has benefited by the labor of individuals whose understanding of the period and desire to see an expanded historical discourse on the arts is preeminent. There has been no greater guardian of the work of Henry Simon than his son, Norbert, and Norbert's wife, Shirley. Throughout the organization of this exhibition they have tirelessly shared information, researched facts, provided additional details, and made almost all of the works on view accessible to the museum. Their commitment to history, knowledge and the work of Henry have been the true foundation of this project. Their association with the Block has changed the lives of many as they have become not only colleagues but lifelong friends. In this context, it is a pleasure for me to recognize the importance of Jerome Hausman, another friend and colleague of the museum. Had it not been for his efforts during the past several years, we may never have known of the Simon family or the work of Henry.

Henry Simon: 1901–1995 provides another cause for celebration as it marks the return of Liz Seaton to the Block Gallery. As a former Graduate Fellow at the museum and its former Assistant Curator, it is a pleasure to once again work with her as curator of this exhibition. As one of a younger generation of scholars, she presents the very finest in scholarship, a commitment to research, and a sensitivity to new ideas and to the importance of the museum. We look forward to working with Liz in the future.

I would like to both recognize and thank those individuals who have placed their faith in the professionalism and care of the museum in lending works from their collection to this exhibition. In addition to Norbert and Shirley Simon,

I would like to extend a warm note of appreciation to Henry's brother David and his wife, Lory Simon. Thanks are also extended to all individuals and institutions who lent to the exhibition, including Evelyn Salk, the College of Lake County, the University of Chicago Library, Department of Special Collections, and the Department of Arts and Humanities, Wilbur Wright College. Further thanks needs to be extended to many who have assisted in support, research, photography and preparation. To the Illinois Arts Council, James Prinz, Hersh Simon, Kevin Chua, Mark Fiske of the Fairborn Post Office in Ohio, Mark Pascale at the Art Institute of Chicago, Mary Ellen Thompson, Steve Jones of the College of Lake County, Tim Samuelson of the Commission on Chicago Landmarks, Carmen Martinez of Wells High School, Sonya Griffin of the Chicago Board of Education, Heather Becker of the Chicago Conservation Center, the Rothschild Foundation, Rick Strilky, Susan Weininger, and the Friends of the Mary and Leigh Block Gallery our sincerest appreciation and thanks.

As always, our final note of appreciation goes to those who serve as the guardians of quality and experience at the museum—its staff. This catalogue could not have been realized without the editing, knowledge, and expertise of Amy Winter, Curator at the Block Gallery. Marie McCarthy, the museum's Preparator and Registrar, has, as always, contributed tireless support, professionalism and commitment to the project. Mary Stewart, Assistant Director, Julie Collins, Curator of Education, Joan Mack, Departmental Assistant, Oren Levin and Nancy Saulsbury of the Illinois State Board of Education team, and Block Gallery assistants, Nina Markhoff and Sarah Myers, have all been of immense help in bringing this exhibition to fruition.

Since the type of society—that is, its culture
and life style—into which an artist is born
is already established, the artist has no choice
but to produce the art of that period.
The only latitude left to the individual artist is
quality and meaningful subject matter.

—**Henry Simon** 1974[1]

Because experience is the fulfillment of
an organism in its struggles and achievements
in a world of things, it is art in germ.

—**John Dewey,** *Art as Experience*, 1934[2]

PLATE 2

Eve, 1929

watercolor and pencil on paper
23 x 16.5 cm
Norbert and David Simon

PLATE 3

Orange Harvesting, 1939

egg tempera on panel

10.2 x 34.6 cm

Norbert and David Simon

PLATE 4

Banana Harvesting, 1939

egg tempera on panel

10.2 x 35.6 cm

Norbert and David Simon

PLATE 5

Bishop McKendree and His Escorts at Lebanon, 1940

casein on gesso with oil glazes

101.6 x 152.4 cm

Wells High School, Chicago

PLATE 7

The Homeless, 1940

egg tempera on panel

22.2 x 38.7 cm

Norbert and David Simon

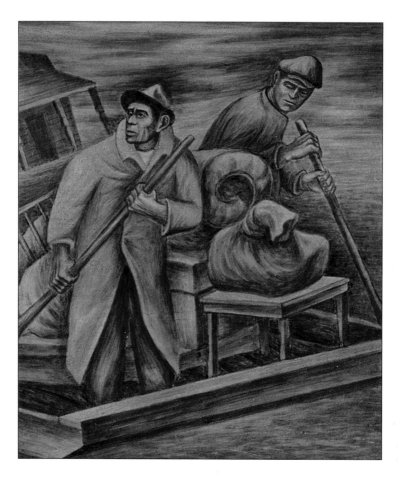

PLATE 8

The Flood Scene, 1940

egg tempera on panel

22.2 x 19.1 cm

Norbert and David Simon

PLATE 9

The Wright Brothers in Ohio (I), 1941

pencil on illustration board

Norbert and David Simon

PLATE 10

Opening of the Stage Coach,
Bret Harte and Mark Twain in Frisco and
California in the Civil War, 1941
Mural sketches for Rincon Annex Post
Office, San Francisco, Section of Fine Arts

egg tempera on panel

17.1 x 52 cm

College of Lake County

PLATE 11

Over the Wilderness Road, ca. 1939

tempera on board

33.6 x 88.5 cm

College of Lake County

PLATE 12

Jesse James, ca. 1942

pen and ink and watercolor on paper

27 x 33.3 cm

Norbert and David Simon

PLATE 14

War Mask, 1942

---

pen and ink on paper

39.2 x 28.5 cm

Norbert and David Simon

PLATE 15

The Artist Observes the Poet, ca.1965

oil on canvas

56.2 x 66.4 cm

Norbert and David Simon

PLATE 16

The Bee, The Rose and The Atom, ca. 1965

oil on canvas

50.8 x 61 cm

Norbert and David Simon

Henry Simon's art closely parallels the story of twentieth-century America. As a boy he was part of the mass immigration of Eastern European Jews to the United States. In the early 1900s, his family settled in a Chicago where a farmer could still keep cows on Division Street. As a man he watched his country survive the Great Depression, the two World Wars, and the nuclear arms race. The city he knew as a youth grew into a sprawling and poverty-stricken metropolis. Chicago's changing faces, the destruction of the human spirit in World War II, the ideological paranoia of the Cold War, and even the growth of Hollywood, found a place in the many paintings, drawings, prints and photographs Simon produced during his sixty-year artistic career.

Simon's greatest public exposure came in the first half of his career, which he began designing posters and stage sets for Chicago movie houses and theaters. Developing his skills as a draftsman and painter, he created work in the popular Art Deco style and made a name for himself and his art. In the late 1930s Simon changed his style, adopting the Social Realist imagery of leftist politics. He became a regular contributor of political cartoons to the *Midwest Daily Record*, a Chicago newspaper affiliated with the Popular Front, an alliance of radical and liberal democratic organizations active in politics and culture throughout the decade. By the early 1940s, as he won mural commissions under New Deal cultural programs, Simon's work turned to folklore and historical subjects of the American Scene.

The same institutions that provided Simon the security to pursue his creative work also required that he adapt his art to their public-directed needs. Group affiliation dominated the Depression decade, and while it brought conformity to many artists' work, including Simon's, it allowed artists to share their pictorial ideas with diverse public audiences.

The second half of Simon's career, from the mid-1940s to the early 1980s, was a period of greater privacy and introspection. In the last years of World War II, Simon produced paintings that expressed distaste for militarism and doubts about human destiny. This war imagery marked a shift in Simon's art: his desire to explore human behavior led him to shun post-war stylistic trends and adopt a fantasy imagery that articulated his philosophies through allegory and symbol. This choice gained him little mainstream approval, but brought sincerity and depth to his work. In the 1960s Simon's paintings focused on the ill effects of urban living.

He used a camera to document and examine what he referred to as Chicago's "lost souls" and folded these figures into surrealist paintings in the style of Georgio de Chirico and Salvador Dali. The dream world in Simon's paintings became increasingly self-reflective in the last decades of his life. In them, he revisited motifs from earlier work and imbued old subjects with new meanings.

This exhibition surveys the career of an artist who remained constant in his use of the tools of the "real" to imagine what reality might be. Though his work grew fantastic and symbolic in his late career, Simon remained committed to a naturalist aesthetic. As conceptualism took hold in art in the 1950s and prevailed throughout the 1980s, the artist felt increasingly alienated from contemporary expressions. "Some of the far out contemporary art seems strange to me," Simon wrote in 1978, "a far cry from the type of art I was taught in the early '20s. Beautiful paintings in gold frames, hung on plush drape walls and soft carpeted floors, romantic paintings of recognizable life, elegant to behold, to study, to worship."[4] He wrote that his experiments in abstract or non-objective artmaking of the late 1940s and 1970s were merely detours. "I worked on a small abstract today and was a little guilty about it," he said, "thinking I could have spent my time working on something more meaningful."[5] Simon's years producing realist imagery for the Federal Art Project, and the predominance of a realist tradition in Chicago, undoubtedly influenced the trajectory of his work. But the artist also considered realism the mode that most effectively communicated ideas and emotions. In his mind, artistic realism did not connote a facsimile of life, but an interpretation of it. Simon thought the "unrealness" of art—its efficacy as a representation or its power to represent the imagination—gave creators and viewers the freedom necessary to open their minds. "There are people...who are so absorbed in the world of reality, practicality and everyday living that they have no room in their souls and minds for fantasy, fairy tale and myth," he wrote in 1984. "They look askance at anything spiritual, mystical or fantasized, thereby depriving themselves of the pleasure and emotional feeling derived from…creative art."[6] The naturalistic exploration of the unreal became Simon's language for articulating his belief in the artist's ability to comment upon and even influence human behavior.

1

Self-portrait, 1940

—————————

watercolor and pen and ink on paper

35.5 x 28.2 cm

Norbert and David Simon

2

Early

Training

and

Professional

Work

1920s and 1930s

Henry Simon was born November 10, 1901 in Plock, Poland, to Victor and Anna Shiman. His parents were members of the country's working class: Henry's father worked as a tailor; his mother raised Henry and his siblings. A year after Henry was born, Victor and Anna decided to join the wave of Polish Jews immigrating to the United States. The threat of socialist revolution, military conscription and pogroms in Poland, and economic opportunities in America, brought millions of Central and Eastern European Jews to this country in the late 1800s and early 1900s.[7] Victor's brother Morris already had found a profitable life in the United States. Victor joined him in Chicago in 1902 to find work and earn enough money to send for his family.

When Henry was five, his mother and brothers, Max and Morris, arrived to Canada by ship. They took a train to Chicago to meet their father, who worked as a tailor in a plant where his brother was foreman. When they arrived in Chicago, the "Simons" (the family's Americanized name) lived in a dingy basement flat on Potomac Avenue, where "the rooms were damp, dark, cold and infested with rats," as Henry later described.[8] Soon after, the family, which would eventually number eight, moved to a third-floor, three-room flat on Irving Avenue (now Bell Avenue) on the Northwest Side. The working-class neighborhood of frame houses was primarily occupied by Polish Jews,

1

Henry recalled, and a few German and Scandinavian immigrants left from a previous wave of settlement.[9]

The neighborhood provided Simon a feeling of nearness to nature—Humboldt Park was only a mile away and a farm still stood next to the Simon home—while being a part of the Chicago sprawl: "It had a bit of 19th-century flavor," he recalled:

I could run across the street with a pitcher and have it filled up with milk for a nickel. The little old farm couple that lived in an old gable-roofed house kept six or more cows in a barn. I guess the city just grew up around their farm and they just decided to stay. I remember the little red bearded man herding his cows across the cartracks (on Division St.) to a big prairie on the other side, waving a long branch, shouting and running from one side to another. This prairie was the original virgin Illinois prairie. It was my delight. I would lay on my back in the midst of it, with the steady buzz of the insects around me and the city noises in the distance. Here is where the teenagers played baseball on Sunday and where the medicine men pitched their tent and sold

miracle cures for one dollar a bottle, and a little further south (on Chicago Ave.) where Bill Cody put on the Wild West show with Indians and stage coaches.[10]

Memories linking the rural and urban realities of his youth informed Henry's art in later years. Buffalo Bill's theatricalizations of the "Wild West" in the big city, for instance, were the subject of several 1970s drawings and paintings.

When he was 15, Henry dropped out of high school, and his older brother Max obtained a job for him as an apprentice in a sign shop. Max was taking a lettering course in a small school on Wells Street, but World War I had interrupted his studies; he enlisted in the Navy and arranged for Henry to finish the course. Through his lettering studies, Simon obtained his first full-time job at McAleer Show Card & Display Co. at Monroe and Clark Streets. There he met signmaker and weekend painter Joe La Pine, a French Canadian lumberjack who had come to Chicago to study art.

La Pine introduced Simon to landscape painting. The two often went to the Art Institute to view works by French Barbizon painters and such American landscapists as George Innes, Albert Pinkhan Ryder and Winslow Homer. La Pine invited Simon on weekend sketching trips to the Caldwell Forest Preserves and to the Chicago Academy of Fine Arts in the evenings to practice drawing from life. In 1920, Simon enrolled as an evening student at the School of the Art Institute (SAIC), studying life drawing with Charles Schroeder and J. Allen St. John and illustration and advertising design with Carl Hoeckner and Park Phipps. While he never pursued a degree, Simon continued to take part-time classes in drawing and illustration at the Art Institute until 1935. Works such as *Morning Sunshine* (1925), a scene in the city's forest preserves, and *Chicago* (1931; fig. 2; plate 1), a view under the "El" tracks, show how the artist used the city and its surroundings to develop his coloring and composition skills.

In Humboldt Park, where he often went
to sketch, Simon courted his wife Eve Karmazin.
The couple married in 1926, and Eve gave
birth to Norbert, their first of two sons, the following year. Simon's family became an important element in his work. Eve modeled for a
series of watercolors Henry completed in the
late 1920s and appeared again in later paintings. In his 1929 *Eve* (fig. 3; plate 2), the curv-
ing contours of his model's reclining figure
and bobbed hair contrast with the neat lines
of her book and modern shoes; Eve's reading
form is emphasized in watercolor against a
spare, penciled couch. Norbert and the family
house-keeper and caretaker, Augusta, appeared in two color and pattern studies in the flat
and opaque medium of tempera: *Norb in Bath*
(fig. 4) and *Augusta.*

To support his family, Simon continued to
paint signs. At McAleer, he met A. Raymond
Katz, a Hungarian-born artist, who helped him
establish his signmaking career. Katz headed

2

2
Chicago, 1931

gouache and pencil on paper
8 1/4 x 5 1/4 in.
Color
Norbert and David Simon

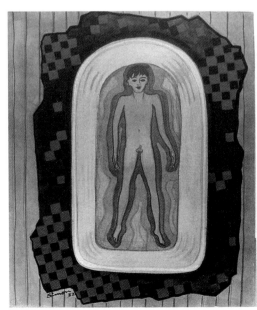

3

3

Eve, 1929

---

watercolor and pencil on paper

23 x 16.5 cm

Norbert and David Simon

4

Norb in Bath, 1932

---

tempera and watercolor on board

40.7 x 35.4 cm

Norbert and David Simon

5

Program design for Balaban and Katz, ca. 1930

---

photograph of original tempera on board

21 x 12.3 cm

Norbert and David Simon

4

the poster department of Balaban & Katz (no relation), which owned a string of Chicago movie houses, and hired Simon as an apprentice. Simon worked with artists in the B&K studio, lettering posters for theater interiors. In 1928, when B&K moved to the Chicago Theater at State and Lake streets, the artist's duties expanded to producing program announcements and sidewalk posters in Art Deco styles (fig. 5). The studio Simon shared with other designers was above a room over the stage. When the organ played to accompany films, as the artist recalled, its booming sounds penetrated the studio floor and walls. H. Leopold Spitalny, conductor of the Chicago Theater Orchestra, gave Sunday morning concerts and furnished music for the theater's silent movies, which Henry and Eve often went to see together.[11]

Simon's work as a designer continued into the early Depression years. He and fellow artist Mitchell Siporin, a neighborhood friend whose family also were Polish Jews, worked together on set designs for local theaters. The collaborations brought the two recognition in 1933 when, as Chicago prepared for the World's Fair, they were invited to decorate a pavilion for the sociology department of the University of Chicago. In the commission, the artists treated the themes of the 1929 stock market crash, unemployment, and the New Deal in a three-dimensional diorama, one of several

6

6

Industrial Frankenstein III, 1993

pencil on board

37.2 x 48.6 cm

Norbert and David Simon

7

The New Deal, 1933

photograph of original diorama panel

12 x 17.7 cm

Norbert and David Simon

produced for the Chicago fair.[12] The panels, which are now lost, represented the New Deal as the capitalist industrialists' defeat by the unemployed masses who had democratically elected a government sympathetic to their cause. One panel showed industry in the form of a mechanical figure or "industrial Franken-stein," as Simon described,[13] being constructed by capitalists, then revolting against them (fig. 6). A final panel (fig. 7) showed New Deal workers planting forests and constructing bridges and housing. The diorama offered evidence of the politicization of Simon's art, which would be markedly influenced by leftist politics during the Depression's later years.

3

The

Political

Artist:

Drawings,

Prints

and

Cartoons

1935-39

Communist leaders in America saw the Depression and its attendant unrest as a vindication of the party's predictions that capitalism was in its final phase. Expecting a workers' revolution, the Party intensified recruitment and campaigning in the United States after the October 1929 stock market crash. The Party's revolutionary agendas attracted many artists and found an outlet in their production. Members of the editorial board of the communist cultural magazine, *New Masses*, established the John Reed Club of New York, which became affiliated with the Soviet-led International Union of Proletarian Writers and Artists. Clubs opened in major American cities around the country, including Chicago; there were 30 with more than 1,200 members before the organization disbanded in 1934.[14] In the U.S., the John Reed Clubs operated "as the focal point for the organization of proletarian culture," as historian Arthur Hughes describes.[15] Members held lectures and exhibitions in workers clubs and organized foreign exchange exhibitions.[16]

Simon became a John Reed Club member in Chicago. Like many artists and writers, he felt compelled to find a way to address the plight of workers and the unemployed after the Crash. As a young boy in the 'teens, he had witnessed his father's support of workers' alliances. He recalled:

He [Simon's uncle Morris] tried to steer my father into conservative thinking since he was a foreman and an establishment man. When his shop went out on strike for union recognition he told my father not to join the union. But my father had pressure from fellow workers also, and decided to follow the workers. Soon after he was caught by company goons and beaten up. When he came home with a bloodied head, I remember him saying to Ma in Yiddish, "Moishe Labe told me not to join the union." He [Simon's father] always was a union member in spite of my uncle. Years later in 1912, when the clothing workers went out on a general strike, it lasted a long time, and I remember going with my father to union headquarters for food and bringing it home in a sack."[17]

The early years of the Depression further convinced Simon of the injustice of capitalist management and the merit of labor unions, an attitude shared by other artists and intellectuals whose financial insecurity put them—as "cultural workers"—in the same league as labor and the unemployed. After 1933, Eve and Henry began to participate in leftist cultural and political organizations. Eve, like many individuals of her generation, became a member of the Communist Party of the United States (CPUSA). Simon, better described as a fellow traveler (his artmaking took priority over organizational commitments), never joined the party, but he and Eve attended meetings of the Chicago John Reed Club.

At the Club's events, Henry and Eve met old and new acquaintances, including artists Siporin, Todros Geller, Julio de Diego, Morris and Alex Topchevsky, and the writer Richard Wright, members of a corps of cultural leftists in the city. In 1934 in New York, Eve saw Henry off on a trip to Russia, part of a self-initiated educational tour of art in Western and Eastern Europe. The artist reported seeing American works in the former Soviet Union,[18] likely entrants in a Reed Club exhibition. Although the details of the trip are mostly undocumented, Simon's family surmises that he went to Russia to explore it as a place to live and work. Hersh Simon said his older brother wanted to produce art there, but regulations against non-citizens working in the country required his return to the United States.[19]

The tour of Russia and membership in the John Reed Club shaped Simon's artistic production, which became noticeably radical after 1934. The Club focused on idealized socialist content and form for the art it solicited from members. Works that displayed "militancy" or "revolutionary" energy were prized by reviewers of Club exhibitions.[20] Anti-capitalist scenes of oppressed workers were produced alongside portrayals of workers united in revolutionary action. Because of their accessibility, prints and cartoons won the endorsement of Reed Club reviewers as suitable revolutionary art forms. Simon adopted this leftist valuation of printed media. In 1937, he began to work heavily in lithography. In 1938, he became the page four political cartoonist for the *Midwest Daily Record*.

The *Daily Record*, founded in February 1938 and published through 1939, aligned itself with the Popular Front. In 1934, the Comintern in the USSR decided that the rise of German Chancellor Adolf Hitler and fascism were an even greater threat to proletarian goals than capitalism. Inaugurated at the Seventh World Congress of the Communist International in August 1934, the Popular Front called for alliances with Western democratic parties to act in common defense against fascism. Earl Browder, the American Party's general secretary, began organizing liberal and socialist organizations in the U.S. to support the PF's anti-fascist and pro-democratic campaign. The John Reed Clubs disbanded and in their place in 1936 emerged the American Artists' Congress, a PF organization whose more broadly based membership of visual artists grew to around 900.[21] Simon's cartoons for the *Daily Record* supported its editorial positions, which verbally attacked the PF's perceived enemies on international, national and local levels. Among the *Daily Record*'s targets were Adolf Hitler, newspaper publisher William Randolph Hearst (leader of what the paper described as the "fascist" or "Tory" media monopoly), and Chicago's Democratic mayor, Edward J. Kelly, whose aggressive and corrupt politics the newspaper frequently condemned.

Simon's cartooning was greatly influenced by the work of William Gropper, a prominent radical political cartoonist of the 1930s. Gropper's reputation was bolstered by successful exhibitions of his paintings at the American Contemporary Artists (A.C.A.) Galleries in New York and by the 1935 *Vanity Fair* publication of *Not on Your Tintype*, a series of caricatures of world figures. Gropper contributed to *New Masses*, which Simon read, as well as to the *Midwest Daily Record*.[22] Gropper's satires relied on clear symbols and labels and a balance of tones (fig. 8), stylistic approaches Simon admired and employed in such images as his 1938 critique of the *Chicago Tribune's* support of Wall Street (fig. 9).

8

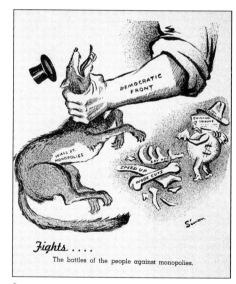

Fights . . . .
The battles of the people against monopolies.

9

Among the subjects covered exhaustively by the *Daily Record* was the Spanish Civil War. Fighting had erupted in July 1936 between a Republican coalition of Communists, Socialists and other radicals, and a Nationalist coalition of conservatives and fascists led by military general Francisco Franco. The war ended in the spring of 1939 with a Nationalist victory. During the conflict, Italy and Germany provided men and material to the fascist side, while Great Britain, France, and the United States remained neutral. Individual liberals, communists, and radicals offered resources to the Republican armies in defiance of their neutral governments. On the "home front," many artists produced images detailing war activity and propagandizing in favor of the Republican cause. Most famous of these images was Picasso's monumental *Guernica*, a mural depicting the 1937 bombing of civilians in the Basque town that was displayed in the Spanish pavilion of the 1937 Paris Exposition. During the same year,

Simon produced his own version of Guernica's destruction in a drawing showing the bombardment of the city (fig. 10). He also designed cartoons for the *Daily Record* in support of the Republican effort.

The war in Spain entered Simon's artmaking more conspicuously than any other Popular Front cause. It inspired his earliest experiments in lithography: he made no fewer than eleven prints on the subject. In *Women of Spain*, a 1937 lithograph, Simon pictured the effects of the war on civilians, portraying a group of armed women huddled protectively near a demolished home. In an untitled image (fig. 11), the artist showed a multiracial group of volunteer fighters, organizing for an assault, a reference to the hundreds of Americans, black and white, who joined the Abraham Lincoln and Washington volunteer battalions to fight in the war. *People's Front* (fig.12), an image rendered in the style of a political cartoon, presents the participants in the Spanish conflict: a Popular

8

William Gropper, *The Road to Rome*, ca. 1935

**Gropper (New York: ACA Gallery
Publications, 1938)**

9

*The Daily Record Fights...The Battles
of the People Against Monopolies, ca. 1938*

**Cartoons by Henry Simon
(Chicago: Midwest Daily Record, ca. 1938)
Norbert and David Simon**

10

Bombing of Guernica, 1937

**pencil and colored pencil on paper
25.2 x 37.6 cm
Norbert and David Simon**

11

Front-backed Republican worker and peasant flank the image; the Republic's perceived enemies—the army, the landlords and the church—collapse in the center, their political structure crumbling behind them.

Simon may have been exposed to lithography as a student at the School of the Art Institute, but it is more likely that he learned the medium at Hull-House, where Carl Hoeckner, his design instructor at the SAIC in the 1920s, oversaw the use of a lithography press as supervisor of graphic art production for the Illinois Art Project (IAP), a Federal Art Project (FAP) division. Simon probably used the facilities at Hull-House before beginning work for the IAP easel division in 1938. Although many artists in the easel division turned in prints to meet work quotas, Simon appears to have reserved his lithography for the private market and political publications. Lithographs such as *Steel and the Forces for War, Asturian Miners* and *No Passaran* appeared in the artist's

12

11

No title given *(Spanish Civil War volunteer brigade)*, ca. 1937

lithograph on paper
33.3 x 43.5 cm
Norbert and David Simon

12

People's Front, ca. 1937

lithograph on paper
23.5 x 25.1 cm
Norbert and David Simon

13

Women of Spain, 1937

oil on canvas
(measurements unknown)
Photograph courtesy of
Norbert and David Simon

first one-man exhibition at Carl Zigrosser's
Weyhe Gallery in New York. Three of Simon's
Spanish Civil War prints appeared alongside
articles about the war in November issues of
New Masses. The artist focused on a group of
related egg tempera and oil panel paintings for
the government, including *Women of Spain*
(fig. 13) and *Asturian Miners*, exhibited in the
IAP gallery in Chicago. Graphic artists and easel
painters working for the Federal Art Project
were free to choose the subjects of their work.
Simon's leftist sympathies remained a thread in
his government art until 1938. In 1939, how-
ever, he was invited to produce murals for the
IAP and the Treasury Department. The radical-
ism in his work would be tempered by the
restraints placed on imagery in these divisions.

4

The

Government

Artist:

Mural Designs,

Paintings

and

Drawings

1938-42

S imon's supervisor on the Illinois Art Project, Gustaf Dalstrom, assigned him to the mural division in 1938. Simon's first mural commission went up in the Cook County Hospital the following year. Now lost, the mural comprised designs similar to *Orange Harvesting* (fig. 14; plate 3) and *Banana Harvesting* (figs. 15 and 16; plate 4). The final 4 x 16' panels in egg tempera hung in the hospital's reception room. Seemingly incongruous for an Illinois site, Simon's images of tropic fruit harvesting in North and South America invoked the spirit of Pan-American unity then promoted in culture and politics.[23] Pan-American conferences held in the late 1930s between Roosevelt and Latin American heads of state resulted in the 1938 "Declaration of Lima," which reaffirmed the absolute sovereignty of American states and their determination to resist foreign intervention in the face of increasing fascist aggression in Europe. Although less politicized than his easel paintings for the IAP, the Cook County mural was indirectly tied to the anti-fascist Popular Front politics promoted in Simon's earlier works.

The reference to Latin America in Simon's Cook Country Hospital mural was also undoubtedly tied to the circumstances of the origins of United States government art patronage. The U.S. effort was based on the model established by the Mexican Ministry of Public Education, which had commissioned artists to create public murals during the early 1920s as part of President Alvaro Obregón's nationalist

14

15

14

Orange Harvesting, 1939

egg tempera on panel
10.2 x 35.6 cm
Norbert and David Simon

15

Banana Harvesting, 1939

egg tempera on panel
10.2 x 35.6 cm
Norbert and David Simon

16

Banana Harvesting Detail, 1939

egg tempera on panel
59.1 x 73.4 cm
Norbert and David Simon

education program. Among the figures to emerge from the Mexican program were Diego Rivera, José Clemente Orozco and David Alfred Siqueiros, who became known as *Los Tres Grandes*. Their work was enormously influential when the U.S. government began to support mural production in 1933: by then the Mexicans' careers had been established in exhibitions, and numerous American artists had assisted them in Mexican and U.S. commissions.

Like many American muralists-in-training, Simon was inspired by the example of *Los Tres Grandes*.[24] But it was Chicago muralists Mitchell Siporin, Edgar Britton and Edward Millman who most influenced his technique and approach to mural design. As they gained prominence through commissions for the IAP and the Treasury Department's Section of Fine Arts, these artists likened their efforts in Illinois to those of the Mexican Three. The Chicagoans helped Simon as he earned his own mural commissions. Millman, who had worked with Rivera during

visits to Mexico with Britton and Siporin in the late 1920s and early 1930s, taught Simon mural techniques, including fresco.[25] Simon, in turn, offered mural composition ideas to his Chicago colleagues, especially to his friend Siporin.

Simon's only surviving IAP mural is an egg tempera design intended for McKendree College of Lebanon, Ill. The mural ended up at Wells High School in Chicago.[26] Completed in 1940-41, it comprises three panels portraying early supporters of McKendree, which was founded in 1828. The first panel, *Bishop McKendree at the Site of the College*, shows the college's namesake, a pioneer circuit rider and the first American-born Bishop for the Methodist church. McKendree, "nearly six feet tall, with robust frame," and "an abundance of dark hair and keen yet kindly blue eyes," according to a 1928 college history,[28] stands on the property of the college with four pioneer companions (plate 5). The second panel,

Peter Akers' Prophecy, portrays the college's first president, who prophesied the coming of the Civil War in an 1856 sermon. In the image he stands amid the war's destruction (fig. 17). In the third panel, *The Circuit Rider*[27] depicts Peter Cartwright, one of McKendree's most ardent junior circuit riders, a fierce opponent of slavery and as one minister described, a man "who was death upon whisky-drinking, tobacco and coffee." He preaches to a farmer, trapper, woodsman, and gentlemen (fig 18).[29]

The confidence he gained producing murals for the IAP led Simon to submit entries to the Section of Fine Arts of the Treasury Department. The Section, a federally administrated project, selected artists to decorate government spaces through national competitions. Simon acquired his first Section commission in August 1940, when he was hired to create a mural for the *SS President Hayes*, a troop transport constructed by the Newport News Shipbuilding and Dry Dock Company of

17

17

Peter Akers Prophecy, 1940

casein on gesso with oil glazes
101.6 x 152.4 cm
Wells High School, Chicago

18

The Circuit Rider, 1940

casein on gesso with oil glazes
101.6 x 152.4 cm
Wells High School, Chicago

18

19

19
American Desert Scene, 1940-41
_____

egg tempera on panel
144.8 x 619.8 cm
Photograph courtesy of
Norbert and David Simon

Virginia. Simon's image, *American Desert Scene* (fig. 19) was hung in the dining room of the ship. He received $1,260 dollars for the commission, fulfilling a contract that required preliminary designs and all materials related to the mural's production.

In the fall of 1940, Simon entered one of the Section's largest mural competitions for the new Social Security building in Washington, D.C.; almost 400 painters submitted designs. The Social Security Act of August 14, 1935 legislated unemployment insurance, old age and survivors' insurance, and granted states money for additional relief to the poor and disabled. Simon's mural design pictured those benefited from Social Security, including homeless migrant workers and their families, flood victims, sharecroppers and farmers, and trade and industrial laborers. Simon's exposure to the work of Siporin, Millman and Britton is apparent in his entry, which borrowed the Chicago muralists' muted earth colors and use of vignettes of

contemporary or historical characters set in expansive landscapes (fig. 20).

Simon chose some of the Depression's most prominent protagonists to be subjects in his Social Security building design. He selected migrant laborers, for instance, who had been widely depicted in the 1930s, their plight given urgency and their personalities character in the images of Farm Security Administration photographer Dorothea Lange and in John Steinbeck's 1939 *Grapes of Wrath*. Simon showed these roving laborers and their families living in a government camp in his panel, *The Homeless* (fig. 21; plate 7). On the right, men set up make-shift living spaces for migrant workers while, on the left, another man prays for the future of these displaced families. The artist portrayed other sufferers in *The Flood Scene* (fig. 22; plate 8), which recalled the vast flooding in the Tennessee and Ohio River valleys of the late 1930s. In a 1939 lithograph, *Ohio River Rampage* (fig. 23), Simon

20

20

Mitchell Siporin, *Postwar Period–Reconstruction*
from the mural *Missouri History*, St. Louis Main Post
Office (1720 Market Street), 1942

fresco
274.3 X 886.5 cm
Photo courtesy of the
St. Louis Post Dispatch

21

22

21
The Homeless, 1940
———————————
        egg tempera on panel
        22.2 x 38.7 cm
        Norbert and David Simon

22
The Flood Scene, 1940
———————————
        egg tempera on panel
        22.2 x 19.1 cm
        Norbert and David Simon

23
Ohio River Rampage, ca. 1937
———————————
        lithograph
        23.3 x 32.4 cm
        Norbert and David Simon

23

portrayed two weary women watching their home disappear in the river's flow. In his design for the Social Security mural, the artist cast his flood victims as two men on a barge with their salvaged belongings.

In October the jury of painters Edward Biberman, Kindred McLeary, Franklin Watkins and Marguerite Zorach selected Ben Shahn of New Jersey to paint the fresco murals for the main corridor of the Social Security building. Philip Guston and Seymour Fogel were invited to submit new designs for the decoration of the auditorium and Independence Avenue lobby. Simon was among a dozen artists—including French artist Jean Charlot then of New York, and Arthur Lidov of Chicago—who received honorable mentions. The award won Simon an invitation in December 1940 to design a mural for the Osborn, Ohio Post Office.

After learning that Osborn (now Fairborn), was the site of the Wright-Patterson Air Force Base, the artist settled on a depiction of Orville and Wilbur Wright. The Wright brothers had developed their flying machine in the early 1900s in and around Dayton, which is located southwest of Fairborn. Simon submitted three drawings for the Osborn mural to Section assistant chief Edward Rowan. The drawings show the evolution of the composition, which became simplified and increased the presence of the two engineers. This project, in particular, reveals how extensively Section administrators dictated to artists who worked for them. In

24

The Wright Brothers in Ohio (I), 1941

_____

pencil on illustration board

Norbert and David Simon

25

The Wright Brothers in Ohio, Fairborn
(formerly Osborn) Post Office, 1941

_____

oil on canvas

182.9 x 365.8 cm

Photograph courtesy of

Norbert and David Simon

February, Rowan wrote Simon that in the case
of the first design (fig. 24; plate 9).

[T]he feeling of the Section is that you can
organize the subject in a somewhat more con-
vincing way and particularly in relation to the
wall. The figure on the right is not convincingly
seated or standing. The scale of the plane on
the right is much too large as it gives the im-
pression of a great ship rather than the flimsy
type of plane which these men first used. The
material right of the figures seems crowded
and chaotic. The landscape on the right should
be set back farther into the composition.[30]

The final drawing was approved in April and
the mural, produced in oil on canvas, completed in September. In the image (fig. 25), the
brothers loom behind objects that guided their
construction of the airplane: the wind tunnel
designed to acquire aeronautic data, an instru-
ment for carving propellers, and a sewing
machine used to produce wings coverings.
Orville, on the right, is shown as the mechanic,
and Wilbur, on the left, as the pilot of the first
successful airplane flight. In the background are

the brothers' first successful glider and their
camp at Kitty Hawk. Rowan wrote to Simon
on September 18 that he was pleased by the
image, but "a little bit surprised to find the
emphasis placed on the hands in enlarging them
to distorted proportions. It occurs to me that
this is a kind of crystal ball distortion which has
been used only in relation to this one feature,
and it seems unnecessarily affected to me.
I question the acceptance of this mannerism by
the citizens of Osborn."[31] Simon had perhaps
enlarged the hands in admiration of Siporin's
tendency manipulate figures in this way. The
technique lent the image the quality of being
dramatically foreshortened. The mural—large
hands and all—was accepted and installed
in Osborn by Simon and Eve in the winter of
that year.[32]

Perhaps the largest mural design under-
taken by Simon for the Section was his entry
with Chicago artist Arthur Lidov to the 1941
competition to decorate the Rincon Annex Post

24

25

Office in San Francisco, California. Simon and
Lidov composed egg tempera sketches for 27
panels detailing the early settlement and history
of the state. The artists focused on California's
colonial history from its 16th-century exploration by the Spanish Conquistadors to its Yankee
engagement (siding with the North) in the Civil
War. Panel studies, envisioned to cover six
walls of the post office, include a portrayal of
Don Juan Bautista de Anza and the Franciscan
Fathers leading the first overland expedition to
explore and settle the region of San Francisco
in the 1770s (fig. 26). A final painting (plate 10)
portrays Bret Harte and Mark Twain, contribu-
tors to San Francisco's early publications,
alongside participants in the Civil War. Simon's
designs for the Rincon Annex project, like his
Social Security building entries, were indebted
to Siporin, Millman and Britton, especially in
their use of earth tones and arrangement of
figures. Siporin also appears to have quoted
elements of Simon's Rincon Annex mural design in his 1941-42 St. Louis Post Office mural:
Siporin's Union soldiers in the panel *Postwar
Period—Reconstruction,* their eyes shaded by
caps, strike the same crouching posture, for
instance, as Simon's Rincon Annex soldiers
(figs. 28 and 29).

A mural design produced by Anthony
Refregier won the Rincon Annex competition,
which drew 82 entries. Refregier's critical por-

26

26
De Anza Establishing San Francisco, 1941

egg tempera on panel
17.1 x 18.4 cm
Norbert and David Simon

27
*Opening of the Stage Coach,
Bret Harte and Mark Twain in Frisco and
California in the Civil War,* 1941

egg tempera on panel
17.1 x 52 cm
College of Lake County

28
California in the Civil War (detail), 1941

egg tempera on panel
60.6 X 61 cm
Norbert and David Simon

29
Mitchell Siporin, *Post-War Period:
Reconstruction* (detail), 1942

fresco
274.3 x 886.5 cm
Photo courtesy of the
St. Louis Post Dispatch

27

trayal of events in California and San Francisco history (panels covered mob violence, racism and labor conflicts, including the 1934 water-front strike) found favor among the Treasury Department-appointed jurors.[33] Simon's and Lidov's proposal for the Rincon Annex Post Office received honorable mention as did eight other entries. The recognition brought Simon a commission the next year to produce a mural for the DeQueen, Arkansas Post Office. Working with the postmaster and state forestry commission, Simon produced *Wildlife Conservation in Arkansas* (fig. 30), showing two men from the logging industry (alluded to by the fire lookout tower in the background) engaged in efforts to preserve the state's fish and birds.

Simon's loss of the Rincon Annex Post Office competition to a design that declared its ideological allegiances to the left testifies to the change in his work by 1942. Section mural commissions led Simon to anticipate the desires

28

29

30

of juries and administrators and this no doubt influenced his selections of subjects. Section art, in particular, was more conservative than that of the FAP, as art historian Matthew Baigell writes: "Because mural competitions for the Section had to comply with local preferences and had also to gain final approval in Washington, artists tended to pursue an inoffensive middle ground of style and content."[34] Although Simon remained politically active as a member of the Artist's Union, helping to support its campaigns for job security, after 1939 he leaned away from the leftist subjects that had attracted him during his first years with the FAP and turned to nostalgic American Scene subjects of local history and folklore that his muralist colleagues were adopting.

In work produced during the early 1940s for both government divisions, Simon focused on stories and myths associated with the frontier. In *Over the Wilderness Road* (fig. 31; plate 11), a design for a mural that was never realized, Simon dramatically envisions the migratory path of early pioneers through the Cumberland Gap and into Kentucky by way of the "Wilderness Road." The image shows colonists from east of the Alleghenies led by a band of "long Hunters from the Yadkin Valley."[35] In the lower right of the painting, the artist pictures the bones of a mastodon from the prehistoric Kentucky plains. In the distance on the left he shows a herd of bison moving slowly and serenely out of the territory while a new civilization, signified by the traders and pioneers, moves in. Simon's image portrays the pioneers in the conventional posture of the faithful and hardened, plowing forward to claim their ownership of the territory. Holly-

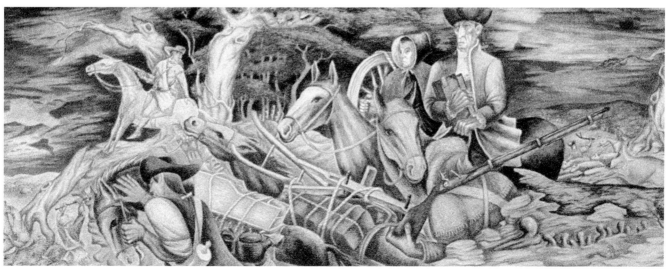

wood productions during the late 1930s and early 1940s fueled the artist's interest in the West shaped the romantic scenes he portrayed in his work. Simon's "ideas" files for art included stills from such films as Cecil DeMille's *The Plainsman* (1936), Henry King's *Jesse James* (1939), and William Wellman's *Buffalo Bill* (1944) all published in *Life* magazine. Jesse James appears in a Simon watercolor of 1942 (fig. 32; plate 12) that likely refers to the country's first train robbery, a holdup of the Rock Island express by the James' Boys at Adair, Iowa, in 1873. Western idols over the years would evolve in Simon's work from Hollywood carbon copies to subjects of more critical assessment. In his 1970 *Buffalo Bill's Wild West* (fig. 33), Simon emphasized the false and performative nature of William F. Cody's vision of the West, picturing Cody as an actor on a merry-go-round stage watched by an audience of cowboys and Native Americans, the seeming judges of his elaborate story-telling.

32

32

Jesse James, ca. 1942

pen and ink and watercolor on paper

27 x 33.3 cm

Norbert and David Simon

33

Untitled *(Buffalo Bill's Wild West Show)*, 1975

oil and pen and ink on board
40.3 x 50.8 cm
Norbert and David Simon

34

Escape of Billy the Kid, 1942

lithograph on paper
27.3 x 32.4 cm
Norbert and David Simon

33

34

Perhaps the artist's most frequently portrayed subject was Billy the Kid, who appears in several drawings and prints from 1942-43. Simon's Kid images partly were inspired by a romantic *Life* photo essay showing the New Mexican territory where the outlaw committed his crimes. But Simon's designs distort the romantic Hollywood picture of the Kid riding off into the sunset. In *The Escape of Billy the Kid* (fig. 34), the artist shows the Kid as a centaur, symbol of man's darker nature, staging a violent escape from prison.

The Kid's persona as animal or "id" and the nightmarish setting of his escape—the prison signified by a small ruin and an abandoned card game—hint at Simon's growing interest in European surrealism in the early 1940s. After the U.S. entered World War II, the disturbed psychic world of the surrealists would come to dominate Simon's pictorial style.

5

Representing

War:

Prints,

Drawings and

Paintings

1940s

World War II ended the Federal Art Project, which was shut down except for a few departments reorganized to contribute to the war effort. Most Chicago artists employed by the IAP were fired by 1943. Some artists joined the military while others took jobs related to the war effort in local industries. Mitchell Siporin served in North Africa and Italy, contributing drawings and watercolors to the Army's circulating exhibitions back in the States. Misch Kohn and Max Kahn became draftsman for the Pressed Steel Car Company south of Chicago, which produced the M-12 tank.[36] Simon, whose job was cut in 1942, found work producing signs at Stensgaard Displays, and continued to produce art privately.

Simon's most public contribution to the war effort were lithographs he submitted to the "Artists for Victory" exhibitions, which opened at the New York Metropolitan Museum of Art in 1942 and circulated around the country for two years. The artist's *Asturian Miners*, from his Spanish Civil War series, was accepted by the 1942 exhibition jury. *Three Horsemen* (fig. 35), accepted in 1943, complied with the organizers' call for portrayals of the "enemy." *Three Horsemen*'s subject and composition were modeled on Albrecht Dürer's well-known woodcut of 1497-98, the *Four Horsemen of the Apocalypse*. Simon had turned to Dürer's print a few years earlier for the design of a political cartoon for the *Daily Record* (fig. 36). The newspaper image showed four figures riding on the winds of

35

35
The Three Horsemen, 1937

lithograph
22.5 x 32.7 cm
Norbert and David Slmon

36
The Fascist Four Horsemen,
Midwest Daily Record, April 12, 1938

Reprinted in *Cartoons by Simon*
(Chicago: Midwest Daily Record,
ca. 1938)

Exposes . . . .
The real enemies of the American people.

36

fascist ideology: publisher William Randolph Hearst; Father Charles Edward Coughlin, the "radio priest"; Irénée du Pont, organizer of the conservative industrialist organization, the Liberty League; and financier J.P Morgan. Simon's "Artist's for Victory" image amended the Dürer composition, including only three horsemen, the leaders of the Axis. The print shows Hitler, arm extended in salute; Hirohito, emperor of Japan; and Mussolini, who holds the *fasces* ax enclosed in a bundle of wooden rods, an emblem of Roman magistrates that signified their authority to scourge and behead. The three dictators in the print are silhouetted against a stormy sky. They ride "roughshod over the land," the artist wrote, waving the Nazi flag and "spreading death and destruction."[37]

In contrast to these images' patriotic presentation of war, clearly defining allies and enemies, private images Simon produced between 1938 and 1948 express anxiety and ambivalence about military aggression. Con-

cern for his brother Max, then serving in the Navy in Turkey, Alaska, Panama and the South Pacific, may account for the pacifist sentiment of these works. Another factor might have been the artist's association with Communist Party organizations: the CPUSA supported the U.S. entrance into the war only after Hitler invaded the Soviet Union in June 1941. Simon's personal portrayals of military battles emphasize not heroism but devastation—the images are in this sense very different from his pro-Republican prints and paintings of the Spanish Civil War. *Landscape*, 1939 (fig. 37; plate 13), shows a desolate bunker in the aftermath of an anonymous battle, the sky and muddy land contrasted with a field of stripped and broken trees. *Everything is Up in the Air* from 1942 (fig. 38), an image revealing Simon's growing surrealistic sensibilities, parodies battle with its cast of fanciful flying machines—a ship, a propeller-driven balloon and a multi-ped cloud—hovering over a smouldering civilization. The title wittily alludes

37

37

Landscape, 1939

gouache on paper
34.3 x 50.8 cm
Norbert and David Simon

38

Everything is Up in the Air, 1942

pencil, ink and watercolor on paper
21.7 x 21.9 cm
Norbert and David Simon

38

to the war's air assaults and the uncertainty of their outcome. In 1942, even as German Field Marshal Erwin Rommel conquered North Africa, the German offensive in Russia ground to a halt. Allied and Axis forces were approaching an impasse.

The most stunning of Simon's images from this period are the war mask paintings and drawings of 1942, which emulate dada and surrealist efforts to transform the meaning of objects by embellishing them or changing their context. Simon's faces derive from his studies of African and South Sea masks in the Field Museum and the diverse gas mask styles he saw in publications during the war (fig. 39).[38] The mask series is also likely modeled after similar visual metaphors invented by the Parisian surrealists to signify the primitivism of modern technological warfare and civilization.[39] *War Mask* (fig. 40; plate 14), for instance, combines the patterns of tribal design and the attributes of modern technology into symbols of the ritual of war and the convention of "primitive" aggressive behavior. The religious conflict—Christian against Jew—that underscored fascist ideology becomes the theme of a related image, *Jesus in Abstract* (fig. 41), which shows Christ as a mask. The image offers several interpretations: it is a condemnation of the National Socialist use of the Christian religion as a "mask" of legitimacy for the atrocities against Jews, or the bewildered face of Christ at the moment of his confrontation with sinful humanity.

39

39

"French Fashion," Midwest Daily Record, August 5, 1939, page 1

Photograph courtesy of
Wisconsin State Historical Society

40

War Mask, 1942

pen and ink on paper
39.2 x 28.5 cm
Norbert and David Simon

41

Jesus in Abstract, 1942

pen and ink on paper
44 x 30 cm
Norbert and David Simon

40

41

After the war, Simon condemned bellicose behavior in a series of drawings called the "Aggressors." In these images, the artist's masked figures are shown as equestrian warriors preparing for battle. Their abstracted armor appears impenetrable, but their movements are unsure. In *Aggressor* or *Wrong Road to Heaven* (fig. 42) Simon shows two warriors under a vision of heaven: one is a centaur, symbol for the artist of the dark side of man; the other, who bears the wings and halo of an angel, wears the ritual mask of war and carries a matching shield. Though their characters differ they are both warriors. Neither can find the way to salvation, pictorially symbolized by Jacob's ladder, either in heaven or on earth.

Simon's 1940s war imagery helped him to articulate a pacifist position that would become a fixture of his later art and writings. During the Cold War, the artist condemned even the perceived threat of military aggression. In a prose-poem from 1962, he reinvoked the image of the Four Horsemen to voice his fears about war:

"I Hear the Beating Drums"[40]

With a foreboding sense of horror I listen to the war drums in the distance. The beating gradually increases until their thunderous pounding can be heard before the gates of the city. Inside the people of good will are seeking truth and peace, and a way out of this dilemma of the twentieth century.

As always the few against the many—men of peace—thinkers—men of high morals—trying to shut out the thunder of the war drums. The race is for the possession of men's minds as well as their bodies. Will the men of good will discover some miracle, idea, or action that will bring this march to Armageddon to a halt? Peace-loving people everywhere wait and hope.

Outside the city's gates the Philistines beat the war drums and are impatient to attack. Inside the men of good will are searching their souls as well as books to find an answer. Perhaps there are many roads to salvation.

It is said the pen is mightier than the sword—if so now is the time to use it. The Four Horsemen of the Apocalypse are being unleashed again and are ready to ride.

The universal forces for peace must be mobilized before man destroys himself.

42

Aggressors or Wrong Road to Heaven, ca. 1948

pen and ink on paper

29.2 x 36.8 cm

Norbert and David Simon

During the early 1950s, Simon took a break from artmaking to focus on supporting his family. He opened a signmaking business, "Courtesy Signs," at Monroe and Wells streets in 1951, but within the year it closed. Periods of work and unemployment followed. Only in 1959, when he began to work for Advance Neon Signs (from which he retired in 1971), did Simon paint again. By that time, though, the artist had discovered another medium. In 1955, while working as a signmaker for Marshall Field and Company, Simon bought his first professional camera in the store's photo department. Through the camera's lens, he began to view the city and its parks—the same places he had studied as a student—with a different eye. Thirty-five years had passed: Chicago was more populous and its neighborhoods changed. Its buildings had grown taller and areas of urban blight larger. Taking his camera to the Loop, North Clark Street, Madison Street and Maxwell Street Market, Simon captured human action in the architectural spaces of the city.

At first he was attracted to people—a worker on lunch break (fig. 43), children in the street, a blind musician—whose faces and bodies narrated the pleasures and hardships of their lives. The camera allowed Simon to frame and record his subject's responses to their existences: satiated, bewildered, accepting, beaten. With each outing, his abilities to observe human behavior grew. He described a visit to Maxwell Street Market in the fall of 1963:

43

A Negro woman asleep in the shade sitting on a bridge-chair beside a store front. A tin can with a hole punched through the top for coins was held in one hand while in the other was held a red tipped white cane. Hundreds of people trudged by her coming from the market place. Some carrying bundles others with sleeping infants slumped over their shoulders. In the throng were people of all nationalities tired from the day's bargain hunting. A babel of foreign tongues speaking loud and unashamed and seemingly in good humor, some stopping for hot dogs and Coca-Cola. In front of each establishment barkers extoll the virtues of their merchandise, tempting the passers-by to step inside and try on suits dresses or shoes. ...inevitably the tourist with his camera and occasionally a professional to immortalize the scene.[41]

From Maxwell Street, Simon went with his camera to North Clark Street (fig. 44), to follow old men whose idle and spare existences left them little to do but observe those who led more active lives. In Simon's photographs these figures appear isolated from their surroundings;

43
Untitled *(worker eating lunch)*, ca. 1960
———————————————
gelatin silver print
25.2 x 30.4 cm
Norbert and David Simon

44
North Clark Street, ca. 1965
———————————————
gelatin silver print
17.8 x 18.7 cm
Norbert and David Simon

they wander or lounge in the streets and parks, observing the city as if it is boxed in a television before them. To Simon the situation of these men was evidence of urban livings' negative impact on the elderly and poor.

Simon's documentary approach to photography was inspired by the Magnum group, a New York and Paris collective of independent photo-journalists, including Robert Capa, Henri Cartier-Bresson and George Rodger. The agency had originated in 1947 to provide solidarity and support to independent photographers for documentary projects worldwide. Simon's cousin, Bruce Davidson, who had grown up in Chicago and also taken some of his first pictures in Maxwell Street, became a member of the Magnum group in the late 1950s. During the 1960s Henry corresponded about photography with Davidson, who was then gaining prominence with his East 100th Street Project (fig. 45), a series of portraits of people in Spanish Harlem, an impoverished and

45

drug-ridden neighborhood in New York. Simon's photographic exploration of Chicago's underprivileged people and their environs show a kinship with his cousin's work. Simon's subjects' tendency to address the camera directly, an action that lends them greater individuality, reflects Davidson's influence.

Alongside the influence of the Magnum group, the sixties witnessed an increase in experimental or "art" photography. Sometimes referred to as "photography of the social landscape," work of this nature by such photographers as Lee Friedlander, Garry Winogrand and Diane Arbus remained connected to documentary photography while offering increasingly subjective, sometimes abstract, interpretations of American society.[42] Friedlander's photographs of window reflections in the early 1960s (fig. 46) may have inspired Simon, who explored this aesthetic later in the decade.[43] Simon found a wealth of compositions in Chicago's business district: a double view of a furniture store (fig. 47); a hologram-like vision of a cafe at Clark St. and Wacker Dr.; a fun-house mirror portrait of the artist with his camera (fig. 48). Always aware of himself as an imagemaker, the artist often included his shadow in these images, which take on an abstract and even surreal quality in the multiple levels of reality they present.

In the early 1970s, Simon showed his work to Art Institute photography curator David Travis. Travis organized a one-man exhibition

45
Bruce Davidson, Untitled, from the series *East 100th Street*, 1966-68

———————————————

gelatin silver print
20.3 x 25.4 cm
Photograph courtesy of the artist

46
Lee Friedlander, *New Orleans*, 1968

———————————————

gelatin silver print
20.3 x 25.4 cm
Museum of Modern Art, NY
Photograph reproduced with
permission of the artist.

of the artist's photographs at the AIC in March 1973. Critic John Forwalter of the *Hyde Park Herald* reviewed the exhibition and commended Simon's technical proficiency. But he lamented the artist's portrayal of "a soft humanity in a hard world…" "I want to think Chicago is more than that," Forwalter wrote, "that there are, somewhere, streets without signs, doorways and windows that reveal happy homes and quiet grace."[44]

The discomforting acknowledgment of the city's real effects on people described by Forwalter was exactly what Simon wished to convey in his photographs. In their reversed spaces, especially, Simon's camera images symbolically explore the feelings of displacement experienced by the city's urban dwellers.

47

47

Untitled *(furniture store on W. Clayton near Wicker Park)*, ca. 1965

_____

gelatin silver print
26.2 x 33.2 cm
Norbert and David Simon

48

Untitled *(self-portrait with camera)*, ca.1965

_____

gelatin silver print
33.7 x 21.3 cm
Norbert and David Simon

7

Allegory

of the

Artist:

Paintings

and

Drawings

1960s to 1980s

The paintings Simon began in the same decade as his photography continued to explore isolation and dislocation as endemic to city life, but the fantasy world they presented suggested the possibility of insight into and escape from such an existence. In these paintings Simon incorporated the figural subjects of his photographic surveys, giving them new pictorial roles. In the early 1960s, he wrote:

The type of human figure I am aware of today is [the] "tragic man," the one seen in city streets. To capture this tragic man, I use the camera. One cannot just conjure up these characters from imagination. They must be candidly photographed in their entirety. I then transfer these tragic human fragments from the citified environment onto a background of my own imagination, sometimes a sandy beach, with water and sky.[45]

The "tragic" men were the source of inspiration for many works from the 1960s forward. In *Streets of Long Forgotten Memories* (fig. 49) Simon invoked Giorgio de Chirico's haunting and distorted architectural views (fig. 50), in a portrayal of a Chicago housing project. The isolated men in the foreground and children jumping rope are drawn from the artist's North Clark Street photographs . According to Simon, the painting is about the draining effects of urban life, which are visible to the aging, crouched figures, but not yet perceptible to the young. "There is a certain mood I think I captured of people, helpless and beaten by the big city... also of children playing jump rope unaware of the misery around them."[46]

49

49

Streets of Long Forgotten Memories, ca.1965

oil on canvas

66.4 x 56.2 cm

Norbert and David Simon

50

Giorgio de Chirico,

The Melancholy of the Politician, 1913

© copyright VAGA, New York

Kunstmuseum, Basel, Switzerland

50

Simon created dream-like architectural scenes and landscapes in the manner of de Chirico and Salvador Dali throughout the 1960s. His formation of a surrealist style during this decade placed him at odds with art trends in New York, but linked him to an interest in the unconscious and the fantastic in Chicago's art. From the 1940s through the 1960s a generation of artists, including Leon Golub, June Leaf, H.C. Westerman, James Nutt and Karl Wirsum, explored the uncanny and the irrational in their work. Their art was inspired in part by exhibitions of surrealist objects. During the decade Simon began focusing on the surreal in his work, the AIC mounted "Max Ernst" (1961) and "Dada, Surrealism and Their Heritage" (1968), both Museum of Modern Art, New York, exhibitions.

Simon crossed paths with Chicago artists who worked in a surrealist style and likely was influenced by them. Carl Hoeckner, Simon's instructor at the School of the Art Institute and colleague on the Illinois Art Project, developed a form of social surrealism in the 1930s, and was still exploring the fantastic in the 1960s (fig. 51). Simon's surrealist work shared Hoeckner's interest in social commentary. Vera Berdich, Simon's colleague on the IAP and a graphics instructor at the SAIC, began creating a veiled and textured dream world in her intaglio prints beginning in the 1940s (fig. 52). Simon expressed his admiration for "The World of Vera Berdich":

51

52

51
Carl Hoeckner, *The Holocaust*, ca. 1935

lithograph on paper
26.3 x 41.1 cm
Mary and Leigh Block Gallery
Northwestern University

52
Vera Berdich, *Symphonic Metamorphosis #1*, 1969

multi-plate color photo etching on paper
18.4 x 24.8 cm
Courtesy of the artist and
Printworks Gallery

Fantastic dreamworld like images—surrealist in concept. Her subjects are plant and animal life, dreamy figures, old world architectural fragments, other dimension concepts like time—mythology—story book and fairyland characters, with chessboards—and occasionally lacy curtains enshroud trees and landscape... all this combined with the skill and draftsmanship of a master etcher.[47]

Berdich's visions and those of other surrealists provided Simon the pictorial framework to explore what he saw as a humanity increasingly hostile to or distanced from nature and bereft of moral guidance. The artist's early training in the American landscape tradition determined his affinity for the environment and sense of loss over its destruction. "It is with a feeling of horror that the outdoor painter witnesses the destruction of his natural environment, the pollution of land, sea and air," he wrote in 1969. "The outdoor painter feels the loss very keenly. But what about the city dweller who watches his dwindling vacation areas. And

what about the rest of the population. Don't they realize that the very earth they depend upon for life is also being destroyed?"[48] The noise and violence of the city disturbed Simon's romance with the landscape in Chicago's parks and environs. He longed for the quiet places he had enjoyed as a boy. "Our modern civilization hides Mother Nature under a blanket of cement and black top," he wrote in 1984, "as though ashamed of showing the bare Earth."[49] Greatest of all was Simon's concern about the permanent destruction of the earth through misuse or nuclear holocaust.

In *The Artist Observes the Poet*, ca. 1965 (fig. 53; plate 15), Simon drew upon his photography and the surrealist tradition to picture the alienation of humans and nature. The painting shows "fragments torn from city streets," as Simon wrote, that "seem to be rude intruders on the face of nature."[50] Figures of old men and women in the image appear harmless enough. But they are unresponsive and out of tune with

the sensuous spirit of the landscape they inhabit. Only two of the painting's figures commune with nature: the poet who watches the sunset and the seated, blind artist (a self-portrait of Simon whose chair advertizes his origins in sign-making) who relies on the poet for inspiration.[51] In *The Bee, The Rose and The Atom* (fig. 54; plate 16), another allegory of the fragility of the human bond with nature, Simon shows the children of the world endangered by nuclear war. The seated father figure facing the H-Bomb mushroom signifies apathy in a world on the brink of disaster. The television antenna and pair of dark glasses refer to his blindness to the fate of the children around him. The exaggerated forms of the rose and the bee in the foreground juxtaposed with the dwarfed architecture of various epochs symbolize the tentative symbiotic relationship between civilization and the natural world.[52]

Travels to San Miguel de Allende, in the province of Guanajuato, Mexico, in the 1970s,

53

The Artist Observes the Poet, ca.1965

oil on canvas

56.2 x 66.4 cm

Norbert and David Simon

54

54
The Bee, The Rose and The Atom, ca. 1965

oil on canvas
50.8 x 61 cm
Norbert and David Simon

offered Simon an escape from the aspects of technology and urban living that seemed to oppress him. The charm of colonial buildings and the seemingly unspoiled life of the natives attracted many artists to the area. In the early 1940s, Simon's colleagues on the IAP, Misch Kohn, Max Kahn and Eleanor Coen, all had made sojourns there. After the war, the GI bill allowed American soldiers to study art at the Institute of San Miguel de Allende. Simon spent some six consecutive winters with Eve in San Miguel producing a series of drawings of scenes from the city's center. Simon used solid pastel hues to advantage in these images, which focus on the colorful, sunlit stucco homes and cobblestones that define the city's pathways (fig. 55). Working in San Miguel allowed Simon to commune with nature as he had done in his youth. Carrying his drawing board, box of oil pastels and folding stool under his arm each morning, he went in search of vistas, returning to his hotel each afternoon to finish his sketches. "After ten or twelve weeks the walls [were] covered," he wrote.

Friends in San Miguel and Chicago bought several of Simon's pastels from Mexico.[53] But for the most part, Simon sold little of his work. To his dismay, patrons and critics did not come beckoning, even though he exhibited at Chicago's Gilman Gallery and the Jewish American Art Club, among other local spaces.

55
Zacatares St. from Church Yard, 1979

oil pastel on paper
35.5 X 43 cm
Norbert and David Simon

By the late 1970s Simon lamented his lack of recognition. He identified himself with the artist Louis Michel Eilshemius, a turn-of-the-century painter of insular, fantastic scenes, who had experienced recognition early in his career, but died impoverished and unknown in 1941.[54] Like Eilshemius, Simon suffered the isolation that comes with lack of attention from the mainstream art world. And like Eilshemius', Simon's isolation inspired an active, creative phase motivated by self-examination.

In images produced during the late 1970s and early 1980s, Simon—as de Chirico did in his late work—re-examined his oeuvre through symbol and allegory, visiting the territory of the real and the unreal he had created in earlier images, summing up and recycling figures and motifs from these works. *Reading the News*, a 1980 painting (fig. 56), alludes directly to Simon's self-exploration during this period. The image shows the artist, on a park bench, as in *The Artist Observes the Poet* (fig. 53), with protagonists from earlier canvases—the homeless man and the centaur. The symbolic figures read over the artist's shoulder as if to help him see into his past as creator.

The figure of the centaur, dark character in Simon's *Escape of Billy the Kid* (1942; fig. 34) and *Aggressors* or *the Wrong Road to Heaven* (1948; fig. 42), resurfaces in other late works. A pastel from 1979 shows Simon in the foreground of a San Miguel street photographing two cowboys, one in the form of a centaur. Each cowboy represents Simon's perception of the different sides of man, based on psycho-analyst Erich Fromm's notion that every person contains all of humanity within them. One cowboy is evil; one good. "We are all saints and sinners, adults and children, and no one is anybody's superior or judge," Fromm, whom Simon admired, wrote in 1962.[55] In another painting from 1983, *The Jolly Centaur and the Cynic* (fig. 57), the mythical creature has a more complex character. Simon shows himself

56

Reading the News, 1980

oil on board

55.9 x 71.1 cm

Norbert and David Simon

57

The Jolly Centaur and the Cynic, 1983

oil on board

50.8 x 61 cm

Norbert and David Simon

56

57

photographing the centaur, who plays with a group of children in a park. In the image, the camera is the lens through which human character is viewed: the dark, mythical Centaur has the potential to act with malice or to play in a child-like manner. The image's title, which identifies Simon as the "cynic," suggests his doubts about the centaur's—or humans'—ability to suppress bad character in favor of the good.

Perhaps the most definitive paintings and drawings from this period are those in which Simon pictured himself with a nude female model. Inspired by similar works by de Chirico and the Belgian surrealist Paul Delvaux, Simon's images address the inherited pictorial subject of the relationship between the male artist and the female nude. In Simon's paintings, the nude, who often wears a hat, carries numerous associations. She is Eve, his earliest model. She is the conventional artist's inspiration or muse, embodying Simon's artistic

vision. Like the female nude standing over the shoulder of the French artist Gustave Courbet in his 1854-55 self-portrait, *Interior of My Studio, a Real Allegory Summing Up Seven Years of my Life as an Artist*, Simon's model is a partner in his effort to recall and evaluate the world he has envisioned in his art.

In *Night Scene* from 1980 (fig. 58), with model on his arm and paint box in hand, the artist walks along a San Miguel-like avenue, the symbo- lic pathway of his career. The figures appear again in the middleground of the painting, a pictorial device that suggests the passage of time. The fragmentary statue in the foreground, a reference to de Chirico's painting, carries associations of ancient culture to which Simon is heir as an artist. The statue also recalls the classical methods in which Simon was trained (drawing the human figure from plaster casts was still prevalent at the School of the Art Institute in the late 1920s). In *Night Scene*, Simon walks away from the

lifeless statue with its antithesis by his side, declaring his commitment to the portrayal and interpretation of contemporary life. In her role as Eve, the model by Henry's side also garners recognition as the artist's inspiration and support. He once wrote, "I would like to have it known that my wife, Eve, is a very important part of my painting process...the pictures turn out better because of her severe and honest advice."[56]

58

58

Night Scene, 1980

oil on board

50.8 x 61 cm

Norbert and David Simon

As he grew older, Simon focused in his work not only on inner human qualities, but also on physical being. In an untitled work from 1983 (fig. 59), the artist presents the phases of life as a garden of statues. Each statue ages further in appearance; the oldest looks away from the viewer. In the foreground stands a young man, the artist in his youth. In 1978, Simon began to lose his eyesight to glaucoma. His hands began to shake. "One learns to accept this as the price of old age," he wrote in 1982, but his paintings suggest he had difficulty adjusting to physical deterioration. In *Street Scene on TV* from 1981 (fig. 60), the artist and his model again walk down San Miguel de Allende paths. In the foreground, a television displaying their image symbolizes a debased, uncreative world. As age inhibited Simon's vitality, the television beckoned, but he abhorred its attraction. "The endless noise of T.V., endless chatter, endless talk that becomes chatter, music that becomes unmusic," he wrote in 1980. "One must muster courage to escape or fall victim to T.V. mesmerization. One must have the will to turn off the T.V.—walk away from it—pick up a book—start writing— start singing—dance—discover self expression."[57] Blindness and age compelled Simon to reduce his output in the last years of his life. In anticipation of an exhibition, he organized his unsold work and documented his career in writing. In 1987, the College of Lake County Community Gallery of Art organized an exhibition of the artist's Depression-era work. In 1995, during preparations for the Block Gallery retrospective, both Henry and Eve died.

By the end of his career Simon had developed a concept of the artist-humanist whose
resistance to civilization's destructiveness devel-
ops into a relationship with nature that can lead
to a model of universal ethical behavior. As early
as the 1960s, he had begun to reflect on this
notion. He wrote about his distrust of capitalism
and support of communism in the 1930s, decid-
ing that neither system could offer solutions or
harmony in the post-Holocaust, nuclear age.
"Only ideas and thoughts based on universal
ethical principles can ultimately lead to universal
justice," the artist wrote. "There is now enough
scientific know-how to feed, clothe and house
the world, but to realize these goals the mind
of man must be guided toward the next and
most difficult step, to desire moral, ethical and
esthetic values."[58] For Simon, the pursuit of
knowledge and creativity would end the waste
and destruction that suppressed human potential. These ideals motivated his artmaking and
informed his life in all its phases.

59

59
Untitled, 1983

oil on board
61 x 76.2 cm
Norbert and David Simon

60
Street Scene on TV, 1981

oil on board
55.9 x 71.1 cm
Norbert and David Simon

CONCLUSION

Notes

1 Simon journal, November 1, 1974, Simon Family Papers, Evanston, Ill.

2 John Dewey, "The Life Creature," *Art as Experience* (New York: Capricorn Books, 1958), 19.

3 I am most grateful to Norbert and Shirley Simon, Hersh Simon, David Mickenberg and Amy Winter of the Block Gallery, Mark Fiske of the Fairborn Post Office in Ohio, Mark Pascale of the Art Institute of Chicago, Tim Samuelson of the Commission on Chicago Landmarks, Mary Ellen Thompson, Steve Jones of the College of Lake County Community Gallery of Art, Carmen Martinez of Wells High School, Sonya Griffin of the Chicago Board of Education, Heather Becker of the Chicago Conservation Center, Susan Weininger, and, finally, my husband Andy Badeker, for assisting in my research and writing.

Thanks also to the staffs of VAGA and Art Resource of New York, the Saint Louis Post-Dispatch, the Museum of Modern Art, New York, the State Historical Society of Wisconsin, artists Bruce Davidson and Lee Friedlander, and James Prinz for providing photography for the essay.

4 Simon journal, September 28, 1978, Simon Family Papers.

5 Simon journal, April 30, 1979, Ibid.

6 Simon journal, May 18, 1984, Ibid.

7 David M. Brownstone, Irene M. Franck, Douglass L. Brownstone, *Island of Hope, Island of Tears* (New York: Viking Penguin Books, 1986).

8 Simon journal, October 20, 1978, Simon Family Papers.

9 Simon journal, October 20 and 21, 1978, Ibid.

10 Simon journal, August 17, 1979, Ibid.

11 Simon journal, October 25, 1978, Ibid.

12 "General Exhibits and Buildings: Dioramas," *Official Book of the Fair* (Chicago: The Cuneo Press, Inc. and A Century of Progress, Inc., June-November, 1933); The circumstances of the Simon-Siporin diorama commission have not been verified by University of Chicago records.

13 Interview with Henry and Eve Simon, February 9, 1995, Chicago.

14 Cecile Whiting, *Antifascism in American Art* (New Haven: Yale University Press, 1989), 21.

15 Arthur Hughes, "Proletarian Art and the John Reed Clubs, 1928-35" (M.A. thesis, Hunter College, 1970): 30.

16 Ibid., 40.

17 Simon journal, October 22, 1978, Simon Family Papers.

18 Interview with Henry and Eve Simon, February 9, 1995.

19 Norbert Simon telephone interview with Hersh Simon, February, 1997.

20 John Kwait, "John Reed Club Art Exhibition," *New Masses* 8 (April 1933): 23.

21 Matthew Baigell and Julia Williams, *Artists Against War and Facism: Papers of the First American Artists' Congress* (Rutgers, N.J.: Rutgers University Press, 1986), 4.

22 An avid collector of source materials for his work, Simon kept a file on Gropper's cartoons. Simon also met Gropper, along with radical political cartoonist Fred Ellis, in New York in the early 1930s. Interview with Henry and Eve Simon, February 9, 1995.

23 At the 1939-40 Golden Gate Exposition in San Francisco, Mexican muralist Diego Rivera produced an expansive mural, *Pan-American Unity*, which alludes to the historical and cultural ties between the two Americas. The mural now hangs in the City College of San Francisco.

24 Simon's library included books on the Mexican muralists' work. The artist also kept files on the publicity generated by their U.S. commissions.

25 The media Simon used for government mural projects were egg tempera on gesso panel or oil on canvas. Oil and tempera provided greater flexibility than fresco, which required an artist to work at the site with assistants. Egg tempera comprises a mixture of egg yolk, pigment and water that when exposed to air and sunlight becomes a highly durable paint film. The egg tempera technique, in contrast to *buon fresco*, allowed Simon to make adjustments to the composition and produce panels independently in his studio. In 1941-43 Simon taught fresco painting at the Hull-House Art Center and Design Workshops established in collaboration with the Illinois Art Project.

His resume indicates that he was also art director at Hull-House from 1943 to 1945.

26 In the early 1980s, Simon learned that the McKendree College panels were not installed at the college but in the library of Wells High School in Chicago, where they remain. Simon Family Papers.

27 Simon completed his research for the McKendree murals with the assistance of board member R.C. Fox.

28 *Centennial McKendree College History* (Lebanon, Ill.: McKendree College, 1928), 97.

29 Ibid., 98.

30 Edward B. Rowan to Henry Simon, February 7, 1941, Simon Family Papers.

31 Edward B. Rowan to Henry Simon, September 18, 1941, Ibid.

32 The mural now hangs in the new post office of Fairborn (formerly Osborn).

33 The Rincon Annex Post Office mural jurors were Victor Arnautoff, Arnold Blanch, Philip Guston and Gilbert Stanley Underwood.

34 Matthew Baigell, *The American Scene: American Painting of the 1930s* (New York: Praeger Publishers, 1974), 54.

35 "Over the Wilderness Road," Simon Family Papers, 1.

36 Liz Seaton interview with Misch Kohn in Castro Valley, Calif., February 28, 1996.

37 Ellen Landau, *Artists for Victory* (Washington: Library of Congress, 1983), 103.

38 See, for instance, the illustrated and annotated "French fashions," published in the *Midwest Daily Record* (Chicago: August 5, 1939): 1.

39 See for instance, the illustration of three different types of gas masks captioned, *Protection of Men*, in the essay "Aboutissements de la mécanique," *Variétés* (Paris: January, 1930). Thanks to Amy Winter for noting this parallel and providing the reference.

40 Simon journal, August 15, 1962, Simon Family Papers.

41 Simon journal, October 6, 1963, Ibid.

42 Barbara and John Upton, *Photography* (Boston and Toronto: Little, Brown and Company, 1981): 354.

43 Photorealist Richard Estes, who painted numerous window reflections, probably also influenced Simon's reflection photography. Simon kept an article about Estes' work in his files. Simon Family Papers.

44 John Forwalter, "Into the Work," *Hyde Park Herald* (March 28, 1973): 14.

45 Simon journal, "About My Credo and My Work," undated, Simon Family Papers

46 Simon journal, November 1, 1978, Ibid.

47 Simon journal, "The World of Vera Berdich," December 17, 1966, Ibid.

48 Simon journal, July 27, 1969, Ibid.

49 Simon journal, December 4, 1984, Ibid.

50 Simon journal, undated, Ibid.

51 Simon journal, "About My Credo and My Work," undated, Ibid.

52 My thanks to Amy Winter for the ideas she contributed to the interpretation of these images.

53 Simon journal, December 15, 1983, Simon Family Papers.

54 "At the present time I am fascinated by the work of Louis Eilshemius. I identify myself with him because of his being neglected by the art world during his lifetime," Simon Journal, undated, Simon Family Papers. Simon's files contained an article published to announce a retrospective of Eilshemius' work at the Hirshhorn Museum in Washington: Paul J. Karlstrom, "Eilshemius' Pursuit of Fame: A Tragic Story," *Smithsonian* (November 1978): 98-104.

55 Erich Fromm, "My Credo," *Beyond the Chains of Illusion* (New York: Simon and Schuster, 1962). Simon kept a Xerox of this essay in a binder in his library, Simon Family Papers.

56 Simon journal, "My Severest Critique," undated, Simon Family Papers.

57 Simon journal, November 13, 1980, Ibid.

58 Simon journal, "Commentaries," 1963, Ibid.

Checklist

Objects listed are from the
collection of Norbert and David Simon
unless otherwise indicated.

Measurements are given height
before width.

**Early Training and Professional Work:
1920s and 1930s**

1. Untitled, 1921, gouache on paper, 15.2 x 20.3 cm

2. *Down by the River*, 1928, oil on panel, 30.3 x 40.7 cm

3. *Gypsies*, 1925, oil on board, 40.8 x 29.9 cm

4. *Eve*, 1929, watercolor and pencil on paper, 23 x 16.5 cm

5. *Eve*, 1929, watercolor and pencil on paper, 15.2 x 29.5 cm

6. Program design for Balaban & Katz, photograph of original tempera on board, ca. 1930, 21 x 12.3 cm

7. Program design for Balaban & Katz, photograph of original tempera on board, ca. 1930, 21 x 12.3 cm

8. Balaban & Katz poster detail, ca. 1930, tempera, 31.4 x 24.7 cm

9. Balaban & Katz poster detail, 1929, tempera, 40.7 x 30.3 cm

10. *Cab Calloway*, ca. 1930, charcoal and tempera, 40.8 x 28.1 cm

11. *Orchestra*, 1929, tempera and ink on board, 18 x 30.5 cm

12. *Charcoal Stage Set*, ca. 1930, charcoal and pencil on board, 28.9 x 39.1 cm

13. *Chicago*, 1931, gouache and pencil on paper, 21.4 x 14 cm

14. *Chicago River*, 1931, gouache and pencil on paper, 17.7 x 12.5 cm

15. Stage set designs, ca. 1932, charcoal and pencil on board, 35.7 x 38.6 cm, 34 x 36 cm, 33.5 x 42.7 cm, 33.7 x 38.6 cm

16. *Norb in Bath*, 1932, tempera and watercolor on board, 40.7 x 35.4 cm

17. *Augusta*, 1932, tempera on board, 50 x 40.8 cm

18. *Industrial Frankenstein I*, 1932, pencil on board, 37.5 x 49 cm

19. *Industrial Frankenstein III*, 1933, pencil on board, 37.2 x 48.6 cm

20. Chicago World's Fair panorama for Department of Sociology, University of Chicago (nine panel designs), 1932-33, photograph of original designs, 12 x 17.7 cm each

The Political Artist: Drawings, Prints and Cartoons, 1935-39

21. *Haile Selassie in Rome*, 1935, watercolor and pencil on paper, 25.4 x 41 cm

22. *Bombing of Guernica*, 1937, pencil and colored pencil on paper, 25.2 x 37.6 cm

23. *Expect No Reward*, cartoon design for *Midwest Daily Record*, Chicago, Illinois, 1938, pen and ink on board, 38.3 x 51.5 cm

24. *The Sword Act*, cartoon design for *Midwest Daily Record*, Chicago, Illinois, 1938, pen and ink on board, 45.5 x 39 cm

25. "Cartoons by Simon," *Midwest Daily Record*, Chicago, Illinois, ca.1938-39, brochure

26. *Women of Spain*, 1937, lithograph on paper, 36.8 x 43.2 cm

27. *Women of Spain #2*, 1937, lithograph on paper, 46.4 x 36.5 cm

28. Untitled (Spanish Civil War volunteer brigade), ca. 1937, lithograph on paper, 33.3 x 43.5 cm

29. *No Pasaran*, ca. 1937, lithograph on paper, 33.7 x 22.9 cm

30. *People's Front*, ca. 1937, lithograph on paper, 23.5 x 25.1 cm

31. Untitled (demonstrators), ca. 1937, lithograph on paper, 42 x 42.9 cm

32. *The Miracle of Madrid*, 1937, lithograph on paper, 32.6 x 22.5 cm

33. *The Ruling Spirit of Old Spain*, 1937, lithograph on paper, 33.7 x 22.9 cm

34. *Force of Destruction*, 1937, lithograph on paper, 34 x 22.9 cm

35. *Spanish Civil War*, 1937, ink with highlights on board, 38.3 x 50.6 cm

36. *Asturian Miners*, ca. 1937, lithograph on paper, 34.3 x 22.9 cm

37. *Steel and the Forces of Peace*, 1938, lithograph on paper, 34.3 x 22.9 cm

38. *Homeless*, ca. 1937, lithograph on paper, 33.7 x 23.2 cm

The Government Artist: Mural Designs, Paintings and Drawings, 1938-42

39. *Banana Harvesting*, mural sketch for Cook County Hospital, Chicago, Illinois Art Project, 1939, egg tempera on panel, 10.2 x 35.6 cm

40. *Banana Harvesting II*, 1939, mural sketch for Cook County Hospital, Chicago, Illinois Art Project, egg tempera on panel, 24 x 101.8 cm, College of Lake County

41. *Banana Harvesting* (detail), 1939, mural sketch for Cook County Hospital, Chicago, Illinois Art Project, egg tempera on panel, 59.1 x 73.4 cm

42. *Orange Harvesting*, 1939, mural sketch for Cook County Hospital, Chicago, Illinois Art Project, egg tempera on panel, 10.2 x 34.6 cm

43. *Fruits of the Earth*, 1939, mural sketch for Cook County Hospital, Chicago, Illinois Art Project, gouache on paper, 7.6 x 42.5 cm

44. *Tropical Fruits*, 1939, mural sketch for Cook County Hospital, Chicago, Illinois Art Project, egg tempera on panel, 20.3 x 7.6 cm each (two panels)

45. *Bishop McKendree and His Escorts at Lebanon*, 1940, mural sketch for McKendree College, Lebanon, Illinois (now in Wells High School, Chicago), Illinois Art Project, charcoal on paper, 38 x 54 cm

46. *Peter Akers Prophecy*, 1940, mural sketch for McKendree College, Lebanon, Illinois (now in Wells High School, Chicago), Illinois Art Project, charcoal on paper, 34 x 44.7 cm

47. *Desert Mural*, 1940-41, mural sketch for *S.S. President Hayes* dining room, egg tempera on panel, U.S. Maritime Commission and Section of Fine Arts, 103.2 x 24 cm, Collection of Evelyn Salk

48. *Old People*, 1940, mural sketch for Social Security Building, Washington, D.C., Section of Fine Arts, egg tempera on panel, 22.2 x 19.1 cm

49. *The Homeless*, 1940, mural sketch for Social Security Building, Washington, D.C., Section of Fine Arts, egg tempera on panel, 22.2 x 38.7 cm

50. *The Flood Scene*, 1940, mural sketch for Social Security Building, Washington, D.C., Section of Fine Arts, egg tempera on panel, 22.2 x 19.1 cm

51. *Ohio River Rampage*, ca. 1937, lithograph, 23.3 x 32.4 cm

52. *The Visiting Nurse*, 1940, mural sketch for Social Security Building, Washington, D.C., Section of Fine Arts, pencil on panel, 22.2 x 59.7 cm

53. *Medical Care for Children*, 1940, mural sketch for Social Security Building, Washington, D.C., Section of Fine Arts, egg tempera on panel, 22.2 x 38.7 cm

54. *The Workers*, 1940, mural sketch for Social Security Building, Washington, D.C., Section of Fine Arts, egg tempera on panel, 20.6 x 38.7 cm

55. *The Wright Brothers in Ohio (III)*, 1941, mural design for Osborne (formerly Fairborn), Ohio Post Office, 1941-42, pencil on illustration board, Collection of Wilbur Wright College

56. *Conquistadors*, 1941, mural sketch for Rincon Annex Post Office, San Francisco, Section of Fine Arts, egg tempera on panel, 17.1 x 20.3 cm

57. *De Anza Establishing San Francisco*, 1941, mural sketch for Rincon Annex Post Office, San Francisco, Section of Fine Arts, egg tempera on panel, 17.1 x 18.4 cm

58. *Life at the Mission*, 1941, mural sketch for Rincon Annex Post Office, San Francisco, Section of Fine Arts, egg tempera on panel, 16.8 x 45.7 cm

59. *The Bear Flag Revolution*, 1941, mural sketch for Rincon Annex Post Office, San Francisco, Section of Fine Arts, egg tempera on panel, 16.8 x 40 cm

60. *Captain John Sutter Discovers Gold*, 1941, mural sketch for Rincon Annex Post Office, San Francisco, Section of Fine Arts, egg tempera on panel, 16.8 x 40 cm

61. *The Gold Rush*, 1941, mural sketch for Rincon Annex Post Office, San Francisco, Section of Fine Arts, egg temperas on panel, each 17.1 x 19.7 cm, 17.1 x 18.4 cm, and 17.1 x 18.4 cm

62. *Opening of the Stage Coach, Bret Harte and Mark Twain in Frisco, and California in the Civil War*, 1941, mural sketch for Rincon Annex Post Office, San Francisco, Section of Fine Arts, egg tempera on panel, 17.1 x 52 cm, College of Lake County

63. *Opening of the Stage Coach, Bret Harte and Mark Twain in Frisco, and California in the Civil War* (detail), 1941, egg tempera on panel, 60.6 x 61 cm

64. *Wildlife Conservation in Arkansas*, 1942, mural sketch for DeQueen, Arkansas, Post Office, Section of Fine Arts, egg tempera on panel, 27.9 x 58.4 cm

65. *History of Milwaukee*, ca. 1940, mural sketch for Milwaukee Post Office, pencil on paper, 45.4 x 106.7 cm

66. *Over the Wilderness Road*, ca. 1939, tempera on board, 33.6 x 88.5 cm, College of Lake County

67. *Pioneers Over the Wilderness Road*, 1939, lithograph, 34.1 x 25.7 cm

68. *Dust Bowl*, ca. 1939, gouache and ink on paper, 34.5 x 31.6 cm

69. *John Henry*, ca. 1940, charcoal on paper, 56 x 32 cm

70. *Leather Stocking*, 1941, pencil on board, 29.2 x 20.3 cm

71. *Jesse James*, ca. 1942, pen and ink and watercolor on paper, 27 x 33.3 cm

72. *Johnny Appleseed: Old Age*, 1942, pen and ink and pencil on paper, 41.4 x 17.8 cm

73. *Johnny Appleseed: End of Journey*, 1942, pastel on paper, 33 x 25.7 cm

74. *Soul of Jonathan Chapman (Johnny Appleseed)*, 1942, lithograph, 32.2 x 26.7 cm

75. *P.T. Barnum*, 1942, pen and ink on paper, 17.7 x 44.3 cm

76. *Audubon*, 1942, pen and ink and tempera on panel, 34.2 x 25.2 cm

77. *Horatio Alger*, ca. 1940, oil on canvas, 59.6 x 49 cm, College of Lake County

78. *Billy the Kid*, 1940, pen and ink and wash on paper, 38.1 x 30.5 cm

79. *Twilight of Billy the Kid*, ca. 1940, oil on board, 61 x 50.7 cm

80. *Escape of Billy the Kid*, 1942, screenprint, 27.1 x 33 cm

81. *Flight of Billy the Kid*, ca. 1940, pastel on paper, 57.5 x 49 cm

82. *Capture of Billy the Kid*, 1943, lithograph, 38.5 x 26.7 cm

83. *Paul Bunyan and Babe*, ca. 1944, screenprint on paper, 33.2 x 26.1 cm

Representing War: Prints, Drawings and Paintings, 1940s

84. *The Three Horsemen*, 1937, lithograph, 22.5 x 32.7 cm

85. *Landscape*, 1939, gouache on paper, 34.3 x 50.8 cm

86. *Untitled (battlefield)*, ca. 1939, gouache on paper, 30.5 x 45.7 cm

87. *Everything is Up in the Air*, 1942, pencil, ink and watercolor on paper, 21.7 x 21.9 cm

88. *Memorial*, 1942, India ink and watercolor, 37 x 47.2 cm

89. *Abstract with Numerals*, 1942, oil on board, 16.7 x 13 cm

90. *Aviator*, 1942, pen and ink on paper, 35.2 x 23.5 cm

91. *Jesus in Abstract*, 1942, pen and ink on paper, 44 x 30 cm

92. *Aviator*, 1942, pen and ink on paper, 42 x 31.6 cm

93. *War Mask*, 1942, pen and ink on paper, 39.2 x 28.5 cm

94. *The Future Looks Dark*, ca. 1945, pencil, watercolor and India ink, 22.8 x 21.6 cm

95. *Conflict*, ca. 1945, charcoal on paper, 24 x 26 cm

96. *How to Cut Fowl or Carving the Bird*, 1946, pastel on paper, 42.9 x 30.5 cm

97. *Hand Writing on the Wall*, ca. 1948, charcoal on paper, 35.5 x 37.5 cm

98. *Aggressors*, 1948, pen and ink, grease pencil and tempera, 20 x 27 cm

99. *Aggressors*, ca. 1948, pen and ink on paper, 29.2 x 36.8 cm

100. *Aggressors*, cover design for Masses and Main Stream, 20.3 x 13.7 cm

Documenting Chicago: Photographs, 1950s and 1960s

101. *Chicago Industrial Scene: Near Northwest Side*, 1939, gouache on paper, 25.5 x 34 cm

102. *Humboldt Park*, 1939, gouache and pen and ink on paper, 30.5 x 45.7 cm

103. Untitled (three men on street corner), ca. 1960, 19 x 19 cm

104. Untitled (cafe at Clark Street and Wacker Drive), 19.4 x 24.1 cm

105. Untitled (playing at the Newberry Theater, 856 Clark Street), ca. 1961, 17.5 x 19.5 cm

106. Untitled (State and Monroe Streets), ca. 1965, 17.6 x 17.2 cm

107. Untitled (Wacker Drive and West Madison), ca. 1960, 25.4 x 22.8 cm

108. Untitled (furniture store on West Clayton near Wicker Park), ca. 1965, 19.6 x 24 cm

109. Untitled (Wacker Drive and Jackson Street), ca. 1965, 19.6 x 24.5 cm

110. Untitled (near Wacker Drive), ca. 1965, 24 x 19.8 cm

111. Untitled (boys in street), ca. 1965, 19 x 18.8 cm

112. Untitled (houses), ca. 1965, 26.7 x 29.4 cm

113. Untitled (newsstand at northeast corner of State and Randolph Streets), ca. 1960, 25.9 x 25.3 cm

114. Untitled (man on Monroe Street), ca. 1965, 27.1 x 28.8 cm

115. Untitled (northeast corner of Madison and State Streets), ca. 1965, 28.7 x 27 cm

116. Untitled (furniture store near Wicker Park), ca. 1965, 26.2 x 33.2 cm

117. Untitled (four men on North Clark Street), ca. 1965, 19.1 x 18.8 cm

118. Untitled (workers on truck), ca. 1965, 25.6 x 20.5 cm

119. Untitled (playing on North Clark Street), ca. 1965, 19.2 x 18.7 cm

120. Untitled (worker eating lunch), ca. 1960, 25.2 x 30.4 cm

121. Untitled (surreal reflections), ca. 1965, 20.2 x 24.6 cm

122. Untitled (blind musician), ca. 1960, 25.5 x 24.1 cm

123. Untitled (men's clothing display), ca. 1965, 23.5 x 19.5 cm

124. Untitled (self-portrait), ca. 1965, 33.8 x 21.4 cm

125. Untitled (Henry in fun-house mirror with boy), ca. 1965, 33.6 x 19.8 cm

Allegory of the Artist: Paintings and Drawings, 1960s to 1980s

126. *Streets of Long Forgotten Memories*, ca. 1965, oil on canvas, 66.4 x 56.2 cm

127. *Driftwood and Black Sun*, ca. 1960, charcoal on paper, 37.2 x 56 cm

128. *The Last Hour or Dualism of a Diabolical World*, ca. 1962, oil on canvas, 54 x 66 cm

129. *Rendevous*, ca. 1965, oil on canvas, 56.2 x 66.4 cm

130. *The Artist Observes the Poet*, ca. 1965, oil on canvas, 56.2 x 66.4 cm

131. *The Bee The Rose and The Atom*, ca. 1965, oil on canvas, 50.8 x 61 cm

132. *Centaurs in a Landscape with People*, 1965, oil on canvas, 56.2 x 66.4 cm

133. Untitled (carousel at River View Park), ca. 1975, oil on board, 53.3 x 63.5 cm

134. *Color Harmony in Light Blues and Brown*, 1976, tempera, 39 x 32 cm

135. *Two Plants*, 1977, ballpoint pen and watercolor, 11 x 18.8 cm

136. Untitled, 1978, acrylic and pen and ink on board, 39.3 x 33 cm

137. Untitled, 1976, pen and ink and watercolor on paper, 22 x 19.4 cm

138. *Tower with Three Windows*, from the series *Skyscrapers*, 1976, oil pastel and felt-tip pen on paper, 35.5 x 42.5 cm

139. *Zecatares Street from Church Yard*, 1979, oil pastel on paper, 35.5 x 43 cm

140. *Corner Fountain*, 1979, oil pastel on paper, 35.5 x 43 cm

141. *The Twins in Mexico*, 1979, oil pastel on paper, 35.5 x 43 cm

142. *Reading the News*, 1980, oil on board, 55.9 x 71.1 cm

143. *The Jolly Centaur and the Cynic*, 1983, oil on board, 50.8 x 61 cm

144. *The Lovers and the Elders*, 1979, oil pastel on paper, 35.6 x 42.9 cm

145. *View from the Bridge: Chess Pieces, Centaur, Nude and People*, 1980, oil on panel, 55.9 x 71.1 cm

146. *Night Scene*, 1980, oil on board, 50.8 x 61 cm

147. *Street Scene on T.V.*, 1981, oil on board, 55.9 x 71.1 cm

148. Untitled (revisiting Billy the Kid), 1982, oil and collage on board, 55.9 x 71.1 cm

149. Untitled (artist with statues), ca. 1983, oil on board, 61 x 76.2 cm

150. Untitled (with Norb in Tub), 1987, oil pastel and ballpoint pen on paper, 43 x 35.6 cm

151. Untitled (faces), 1987, oil pastel and ballpoint pen on paper, 43 x 35.6 cm

152. Untitled (self-portrait), 1940, watercolor and pen and ink on paper, 35.5 x 28.2 cm

153. Untitled (self-portrait), 1970, charcoal, 42.4 x 30.5 cm